THIS IS NOT A TRUE THING

(A tragical-comical-historical-pastoral)

Emily Critchley

*Dearest Andrew,
Proof that it is a true thing!
Love, E
x*

Published by "Intercapillary Editions" 2013

Copyright © Emily Critchley 2013
All rights reserved
ISBN 978-1-291-38878-7
IntercapillaryEditions.com

Paintings by Emily Critchley.
Photographs on pages 14 and 27 by Alex Flynn.
All other photographs by Emily Critchley.

This is Not a True Thing

For Edmund!

There will we sit upon the rocks...

Christopher Marlowe

Stumbling on Alchemilla, Cow Slip, Savory (creeping) & Savory (winter)

& it is surprising how it is common
& without petal & laps
over my lady's mantle
too much. Leans into green,
tries to let hope spill over tendrils, a rush
of morning, to keep things bright
like yellows in their waxy virtue (faint
half-flush that dies). The will to re-grow everything
is strong
– divided leaves –
to go back there.
Subconscious squeaks up,
fan-shaped
wth its small teeth:
too late the season, my dear, too late

& so far away! Moving
to open ground is just a ruse
to have us chase
down mountains native to their heights.
But how perennially. The scent emitting diode
needs filling with coin
– of spring –
it is a very cow dung,
tosses back everything we stoke
it in its kept silence;

it's such a sluttish heap. With slip
of heaven,
sudden heat catches

– flowering –
somewhere about here,
where it's
too slow, my dear, too slow

until
the ground creeps up above
& then runs out
for anyone to catch
– over such vast
distance –
huge bee plant of it breezing
low ground cover, daring to try
to savour, *try*
without salt at least, to colonise
& bright green linear.
Maybe an aphrodisiac
for all the summer. Hardy as anything:
frost, volatile, & other
properties. For it is so
nearly over
that harsh winter that was long
& far
too good to go.

The conception of the event after the event runs slowly
thru the cloud cover

Affection makes you false

In animals:
Wait… A third ram runs out of the woods and mates with the female while the two
males are fighting.

Notice the ideal
pattern coloured by that young stag's fur.

I doubt a stag can even fawn
past intellection.

Let's go all out & test it with the Compass
Game.

As in: direction? **Right**! You have found
approximately the number x, i.e. the value of yr valediction
against fucking. Wait, you called plainly ?
Wrong! This would give you the conversion of x into y.
This operation's carried out on carnal lines
& not poetic ones!
Ambivalence is not sexy.

Yes, there's a sign to drive the maidens back
against the trees of forests, yes, to cut off –

Whatever.

The playing distance rules:

Drop all the sticks. See how many you can find.
Look particularly in the bushes. A bird in 1 hand, etc.

This is Not a True Thing

This is so true it might be said to – dying certain
Dis-substantiated. This is marrying resistant & / or
Contrary elements (as buttered ice / unstoppered lurking)
Turned diurnally to prize the point as that (synthetic?)
Distance. This is real heart in here – hope
Fully. Over there is damn hot for the game in which
Certain point grass greenery springing of such,
Points splicing each to each other.

                    My company & I. We listen.
We are a sympathetic bank in thyme for troubles.
Tho still having trouble at your age. Let me sense your
Mouths hurting at the scent of jointure. The dysgeusia
In there, wedded to a formal, a techne – technical trouble. We are
Having a baby to avoid the Plead formal / tick
Ing the box. Precocious weed is category, is dust
Or have you seen another data – all that nasty face-
Punching responsible – My partner & I we know all
The major European cities. We talk so very very very long hours.
Won't be kidded out the space left by anyone's cytosis
– Specially not your common-or-gardener-knees-up-after-love-on-offer Tricksiness.
The hood-wink oxytocin spread to other branches,
Dying the vision cloudy – a jellied deliquescence – a seep outward
Of the clutter. Shush that latter into sex by / crunch those numbers.
None or one into a matter amortised – amor-talized – Desperately Contemn those
paupers the haughty razing seed marker for fair
All down by wall before the fallen's even been noticed.

    & Venus laughed hard upon every one of them

Somewhere in the gathering light rain wooshes to
Flood Somewhere other than guilt Somewhere with
Cloud-gold edges underlying liquid. Here tho is all
The distance you create Here is no shared equity
Or balance at the stakes Locked in a box you know
Well know that I am not one for the transcendental –
Communicate – Telepathy – you know that the waits
Of justice giving her arms to ache. Harder with each
Tho at the feast you sat upon the *dais* with other
Honorable people About weeping and wailing,
With other worthy folk upon the *dais*. All full of joy
And bliss the Error in then dwindling a start. I know
Plenty of dancing & sand piles Cursed gifts & forgetting
The more spent days or of plenty locking conclusions
As time leaks Into a key to sudden chance, O you fickle
That quite equilateral & is there Tho bright was the day
& blue & however the earth beneath purpose gratifying
Clear as the mud below feet. Which maddening water.
Somewhere the hay shoots the grain; the orchard or
Chaff-wheat So merry the month of Spring. & little removed
From depressed things, which is the exaltation of Jupiter.
It so happened that the beams in the eye-lids of flowers
Were gladdened with warmth at the concluded garden
Mild as a lamb, no snap-dragonning, locking of horns
Tho natural Supple as flowers or golden at the further side
Into that gate who with Pluto's wife made delay of

Answering pitched past the best laws of Blindness
The hour waited or in drawing of sword I dare
Well say she would outmatch him. Full of instruments of

Music You getting ahead of your self, the most dainty dances
Never trumpeted half so clear to make trial of her spirit
In such way Traipsing of dated costume. & unsteady among
The Rockery Not even light but blind without say
In your own Firmament; Phoebus pitch'd up at that hour;
Say with agency,
Who is the king of that garden & many a lady with him,

Open Field Poem

You dodged a ladder through the infolds of yr sex
Already there. You crawled thru fields of such
Fleeciness, dropped as loathe to drop it from
Off best as deliberation. You drew a cherry branch
Toward them for an out-of-reach moment, it snapped
Back a hand-me-down to make its own fall softer.
You tried bringing italics to England but you were
Too late. You yawned so hard we'd never catch
You. Two's a company, you said, in the Campagna
Hours. Let's not wait till dark to do something
About it, I replied. You cried open field & generous!
I sighed I know I already felt the lack of them.
You repelled self-interest brightly, using the same
Hands used to brush away others, stamping your
Spread across the table. Lets not eat over all this
Again.

Love & the Debasement of Being
'*On s'est connus, on s'est reconnus*
on s'est perdus de vue, on s'est r'perdus d'vue
on s'est retrouvés, on s'est réchauffés
puis on s'est séparés…'

Our box – a holding
company of outstanding stock
of others. Ticker taped & yet
with increased not diminished
risk. The oil we spread on that,
has scent of oranges, it runs out
hlf way through arrangements,
makes me sorry I told / came.
& yet my love for you, etc. how
frightening. But yrs for me – how
even more. The packing it comes
wth, sections it carves, ready
to be off at all times, whenever.
'Gift it gives, negatively.'
& how I need I take
it to be taken. How melted at
the seams. Wth everything
I have. Any dinner date possible;
no relay or delayed chance /
other real events /
whatever.

One cognizes, re-cognizes,
loses oneself from view, finds
a separation, warming to a theme,

knows that to leave now
may be the only thing to do.

More seriously, regarding such structure

He ran said numbers by me, faded yet still visibly
What is the purpose of such holding counting back
The porticos, the calculations he made – numbers in there;
In to a very sated, stated, simple reasons – have no real
Application. Besides they crunch a simple lack –
Architechtonics – Tho the diagrams hold up alright,
Run heavy down as feather-of-lead or the bright smoke
Thru which the lead me seeing me down.

& yes, such vertical's still hard & not unreal for me,
Tho faded, far from him as
Straight unbowed is. Things stand as they must.
As he was not meant to let me stand it. See how it matches
His eye with its grey intent. See how it won't let go.
That hoisting outwards at such cross purposes
Won't let me let it go.

This Demiurge*

The point is ineluctable, the dying certain; the swan song
An emotional or intellectual distancing – distantiated. I will
Keep the whole together to the point of exit-flying. I will
Segment the fears faster to a flexing of the elbow wing,
An urgent demiurging. Then flight patterns hoist up with their pay
Load from such a height – they are one sith mine happy outlook,
Mine companee, the taxiing out of which is telematic:
Hers, not yours / his / its, etc. I will do none of this
Right. (& mute swans are not mute: they hiss,
& do not sing – are literally 'public workers')
My company & I, we have these stocks to drive the figures
Out by. Fashioned not created, begotten not made,
Of one substance – tho our solace needs are heavy
For the oil leaks such a time, a deliquescence when birds will eat
& not be mopped up as an imitation for. Extra limbs
Someone are needed now. Any one's. Extra dependents
To abrogate the distance gainst the dark we sing thus into.
La la la la la. The snowy dark; the flickering propitious.
Everything at once a bent saw wing – reduced / expanded out again
For flight.

*In the arch-dualist ideology of the various Gnostic systems the material universe is evil while the non-material world is good. The demiurge is malevolent

Precept upon precept; line upon line: here a little, and there a little

What was it we used to like
doing being vain, vexatious
& overmuch? Sing into our fishhearts
littel remedies for stings & other
jelly moulds?
Bring out my replacement! Set her
on the tablet. Curve that
roughly her chiseled jaw – but don't
hurt her as you've done me, no,
try not to do that.

I met a Human Traveller

He was drying on the sands' desert lazily
stretched out, a creature below the monument,
not of marble, paper neither, but a stone
whose touch one fastened on to, traced the history
of haptics, objects & charms, talismans
& Gnostic gems, seals & fetishes from other eras –
all productive of the mess that lay glinting
in the buttered curves around.
Take a pear for that pain. Wait
for mortal shade – you have none in yr heart.

He spoke and when he did powers that moved rock
formations, stratigraphic metamorphoses.
Not so much game as drawn into the fundament,
breaking an entrance to the vaulted clouds to lie
there tonight. Why swear on lifeless things:
mere plinths of minds which take the place
of other substrates; dancing on the firm cave's floor
(when once was swimming to be had). Why else
trip on apples passed, savouring
the blank sandscape where they had to pitch their way
to start again, till fire purge away all things.

The argument goes thus: in the beginning, love
was glorious and the sky equal to the sun
's ruin – almost proper

to a spatial version – then comfort crept in,
took the type for turning. Generations grew
away from bodies: substituting that prehensile
joy for knowledge of the kind that begets clothes,
tools or a steady source of children.

Parity is all dried up. & who loses that
questions. No. Wheat fields are evidence
of moisture. Not so much a hoard as healthy newness,
after the natural tears have dropped and they have wandered
solitary long enough.

The hand that mocks that but the heart is fed. Nothing
beside remains.

First & Last (Cytosis deficiency)

Turning back
for just a wink, a trice, & to check men could,
then drops his angled point, tries that out,
grasps it's a no-go, see him for dust.
The cut the little twist the un-grasp
all intricately caught in him, around him,
over. Never a thought sideways or behind.
Pulled by other things is better & out of sight…
Likes which thistle-like require no
constant, change without light
winds. Objects are not people, but at the start
who realizes. Ha!

Is night-time is lovely. Luck has nothing
to do with any thing. The lock unfastened
out of good will, & but gently. Mute fascination
across lines, & she is somewhat
in the place of others too.
Better to take hold & not to meet… She will diminish
Like the rain. It always does.

Link lizard brain to action, pull away
now. Plan that penthouse box; his empty.
Glad of the peace. So much unwelcome coming over
the transmitter – even without wires.
Yet at night, the melting somewhat,

fumbling ulterior image. Name them. Give it up
river of melted ice – in Summer after all.
Others can cross the mess.

Cue rain & more dirt. Roving eye
cut off from mercy like a heaven.
Draw sand into that mouth – & out again,
a fish fashioning its cozy hole.
Did I give you leave to sure? I did
not. Shoot an awful longing, then sleep
sundry places like the cat that ate
the fish. But for one who knows
not how to nestle,
how to give still,
is that silliness. I mean you.

It never rains but takes the whole season
to learn what's fashionable. Little fish suits.
Background Galleon 6" classic,
Comes in pine. Then loss goes easy,
not as deluge, more a gentle drop or two.

The Nymph's Passionate Reply to Her Shepherd

Take my right wing / pin
It to yr loving cap / feathers
We will make of it / purposely
To be a-roving wth you / endless
Past the apple plants & furry
Things that snuffle / shake or creep
Which we'll let roam. / The only food:
Sighs of true lovers' bliss / & only
Drink: tears of true lovers' eyes.
My dresses of the velvetiest leaves
Twisted with stalks / in at the waist,
Yr boots of bark. So will we / furnish us:
In our bower of deliciousness,
& like the burr stick here / or there
Or who cares where!